The Conklin Mills and Falls
LaFayette, New York

John Milton Conklin standing in the doorway of his mill

Compiled by J. Roy Dodge
From Contemporary Sources
2016

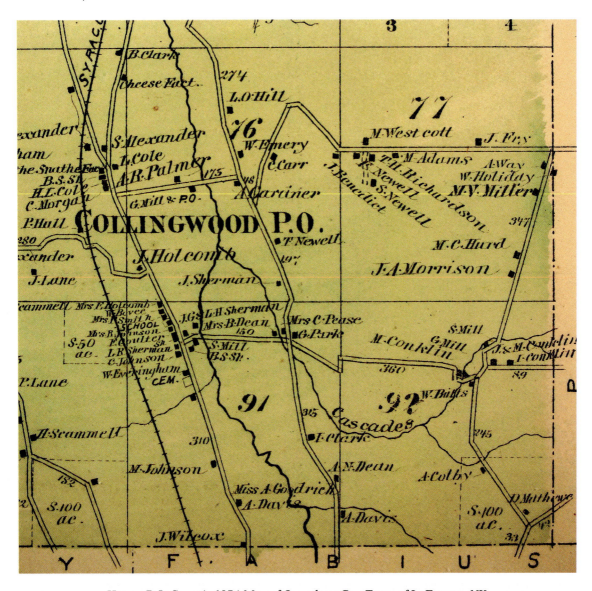

Homer D.L. Sweet's 1874 Map of Onondaga Co., Town of LaFayette, NY

Map shows roadways from Jamesville-Apulia Road, across Cascade Road, crossing Clark Hollow Road and up Miner Hill to the Conklin saw and grist mill and continuing on to the Berry Road. Many of these roads were laid out ca. 1799 to accommodate the mill.

Copyright © 2016 J. Roy Dodge - All rights reserved

Photo-editing and publishing by
Bill & Joanne Casey
Bill5308@aol.com
ISBN:978-1-329-84562-6

HENRY STANTON, PHOTOGRAPHER

Most of the pictures in this publication, with the exception of about ten which are otherwise noted, were taken by Henry Stanton (1833-1910). He came to Syracuse in the 1860's from Massachusetts and worked as a photographer. The City Directory of 1880 lists him as a "match manufacturer". The census of that year finds him in the 8th Ward with a wife and four children aged between three and sixteen. He does not appear again in any directory until 1888 when he was living on West Adams street, no occupation given. The next year he is listed as a photographer on East Onondaga street. From 1892 through 1894 he is called a "scenic photographer". We have two of his photographs taken in 1891 at Cardiff, NY when he was living at Onondaga Valley.

Henry's sister - perhaps his half sister - Florence Stanton was about 40 years old when she came to Berwyn to work as J. Milton Conklin's house-keeper. She is so listed on census in 1900 and 1905. It was during this period that Henry Stanton took the photographs found herein. He gave prints quite generously to J. M. Conklin's neighbors. Those reproduced here belonged to Raymond and Fannie Swift, Homer and Jessie Newcomb, James and Carrie Partridge and to Mr. Conklin himself.

Henry Stanton (1833-1910), likely with his second wife, Mrs. Annie Bessey, whom he married in 1887.

COVER PHOTO: The lower or first falls, by Glenn Patrick Ferguson, July 2007.

Back side of the mill showing the creek and penstock. The wing at right contained the steam boiler added in 1874.

"...To my knowledge, which is taken partly from hearsay, but somewhat from observation, the chief parts of the equipment were three mill stones, one for wheat flour, one for buckwheat and the other for grinding cattle feed. Of course wheat and buckwheat bolts, grain elevators, shafting and pulleys as well as belting and gears were necessary. There was a complete line of wheat cleaning machinery, capable of separating all foul seeds from the wheat with a minimum loss of grain.

One would probably wonder how so small a creek could run so much machinery fourteen hours or more a day, but it did run it with a twenty-four foot overshot water wheel. However, there were times during the summer when the water power was insufficient, so a huge steam boiler and engine were installed..."

(Milton Downing, 1921. From: "The Spirit")

This is one of Henry Stanton's best known photographs of the Conklin Mill. Every inch of ground in this picture has been reclaimed by forest growth. In the wing on the left can be seen the smoke stack for a steam engine which Conklin Brothers installed in October, 1874.

THE CONKLINS AND THEIR MILLS

The first and most important industry for the pioneer settlers was the establishment of saw and grist mills. The first ones in Onondaga County were built by Asa Danforth at the falls on Butternut Creek at what is now Jamesville. The grist mill went into operation in the fall of 1793, the saw mill the previous summer. Every town has its stories of the earliest settlers carrying a bag of grain upon their shoulders to be ground. Here are two, out of several, with local connections.

Ebenezer Hill arrived here from Hoosick Falls, Rensselaer County, on February 14, 1795 to take a look at the land he had purchased. In the winter of 1797 he returned, made a clearing and built a log cabin on the west side of Clark Hollow Road across from where his large brick house was built thirteen years later. Rev. Seth Deleven of the LaFayette Congregational Church interviewed Mr. Hill and later wrote his obituary. In his historical sermon of Thanksgiving Day, 1847 he says that Ebenezer Hill carried a bag of grain on his back "to a mill in Manlius" for grinding. This would have been Danforth's mill at Jamesville, then in the town of Manlius, a distance of about eight miles. In another historical sermon, this one preached by Rev. Avery R. Palmer at the Baptist Church in Tully for the county centennial of 1894, he says: *"In the fall of 1793 a lad of about 19 years by the name of Hall at Navarino, having learned that Danforth's mill was completed, and not relishing the product of the stump mill, took nearly a bushel of corn on his back and went to the mill, over 15 miles distant and returned home proud to have some regular corn meal once more."* (Tully Times, June 2, 1894) All of this is to set the stage for the arrival of the Conklin brothers and the importance of their mills.

These brothers were Isaac aged 35 with wife Elizabeth, known as Betsey, and several of their children; the boys named John D. and Isaac Jr. are known for certain. The other brother was Elias aged 23 with his new wife, Rachael Haight, whom he had recently married in Canajoharie, Montgomery Co., N.Y. They were two of the nine children of Jacob and Katherine Conklin of East Hampton, Long Island. Their residence in Montgomery Co. was brief but they were there on June 19, 1797 when Isaac received a deed from two land speculators for 500 acres on Pompey Lot #92. After their settlement here Isaac received another deed dated Feb. 15, 1798 from the same grantors. This document tells us that he paid *"525 pounds, 12 shillings and 9 pence current money of the State of New York."* Then it adds a particularly obtuse sentence saying, *"in his actual possession now being by virtue of a bargain sale and lease to him thereof made by the said first parties by Indenture bearing date the day next before the day of the date of these presents and by force of the laws for transferring of uses into possessions."*

The biographical sketch of Elias Conklin in the Reunion and History of Pompey (1875) pg. 288 says that he *"came from Long Island and settled in Pompey in 1797. He cut his way through the forest from Pompey Hill making the first road to the place where he built the first saw and grist mills in the town."*

Milton Downing's essay (1921) tells us that, *"the mill existed much as it was originally built until the next generation of Conklins grew old enough to be millers. Then under the fresh vigor of Milton Conklin and his brothers, the mill was enlarged to its present size of three full stories...the chief parts of the equipment were three mill stones, one each for wheat, buckwheat and grist. Of course wheat and buckwheat bolts, grain elevators, shafting, pulleys, belting and gears were necessary...It is said that Mr. Conklin could make 47 pounds of flour from a bushel of wheat under favorable conditions..."*

When the mill was operating it was of such importance that roads were laid out to reach it. The Pompey Road Book tells us that present Chase Rd., *"to the grist mill owned by Conklin...to Mr. Conklin's mill"* had been laid out and was recorded May 3, 1799. Under the same date Berry Rd. north of Conklin's is noted. The next year a road going west was surveyed, *"from Isaac Conklin's grist mill to the north-south road at James Sherman's."* This road passed down what was later called "Miner Hill", crossed present Clark Hollow Rd., went west on what is now marked "Cascade Rd." to the "north-south" road which is

Apulia Rd. By the turn of the 20th century this road down to Clark Hollow had been abandoned and Edna Everingham told this writer that after she came to the farm at that corner in 1914 she never saw anyone use it. At the top of this hill but below the mill was the farm of Thomas Miner and there Viola Miner, the first wife of Jirah D. Palmer, grew up. Another road, now Berry Rd. to the Skaneateles Hamilton Turnpike (Route 80) was recorded January 10, 1801, *"laid out to accommodate the Fabius People to come to mill."* Similarly present Clark Hollow Rd. north was surveyed by Asa Wells March 22, 1808, *"from the foot of the hill on the road that runs from Conklin's Mill to Sherman's Mill and running to Ebenezer Hill's house."*

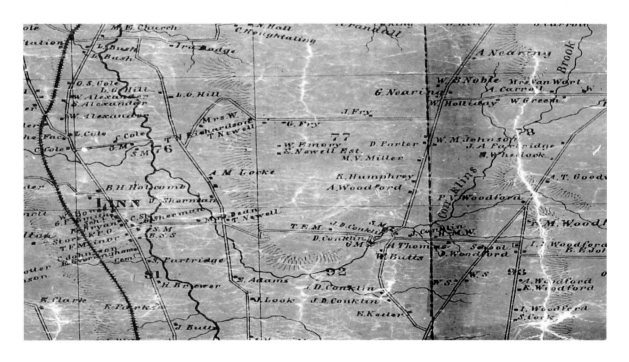

1860 Dawson map showing easterly route to Conklin Mills from James Sherman's in Linn (later called "Collingwood"), over Cascade Rd. and up Miner Hill. The route continued east of the mill out to Chase Rd.

Jacob and Katherine Conklin, the parents of Isaac and Elias, came here after the taking of the 1800 Census and according to Newt King's notes they had a log cabin on the N.E. corner of Chase and Berry Rds. where their grandson, John D., later built a frame house. Jacob died February 2, 1814 aged 78 and Katherine on April 18, 1808. A rubbing of her headstone made by Sylvia Shoebridge is reproduced in Crossroads Town pg. 136 where it is marked as *"the oldest stone in Berwyn Cemetery"*. In fact this honor should go to the stone of her son, Isaac, who predeceased her by about seven months. The circumstances of his death were entirely forgotten until recently rediscovered in the writings of Miss Luella Dunham.

Riding back to Pompey Hill after her visit to Conklin's Falls in June, 1879, Luella tells this story, careful not to mention any names lest a descendant be offended. *"Here a certain pioneer family settled. The husband died in 1807 of ague contracted at Salt Point while chopping wood for the salt boilers. In the funeral discourse Parson Wallis said, by way of consolation, 'It was God's will. God's will. God's will must be done, therefore he died, and he would be happier in heaven than on earth!' Thereupon the widow declared, 'Twa'nt no sich thing. If he hadn't went to that pesky place, Salt Pint, and caught the ager, he'd be alive now. God didn't have nothing to do about it!"* Luella did not need to tell us the man's name for she has given one indispensable fact. He had died in 1807. Going to the Berwyn Cemetery list there is only one possibility—Isaac Conklin who died September 29, 1807 aged 45. But suppose her man had been buried in an unmarked grave? Here the unique collection of Pompey Historian Emeritus Sylvia Shoebridge confirms the story. Found therein is a transcript of the diary of Rev. Hugh Wallis, minister of the Congregational Church at Pompey Hill. Notice that Isaac died on Sept. 29th. By the time his body was brought from Salt Point, now the north side of Syracuse, and buried it was October and Rev. Wallis recorded, *"October, 1807—attended the funeral of Mr. Conklin"*. By "attended" he meant that he had preached the funeral sermon.

In 1980 Sylvia Shoebridge did extensive research among the Conklin deeds in preparation for her tour of the mill site and the Elias Conklin house then occupied by VanBergen and Ruth Smith. The mill had obviously been built during 1798 for by a deed of January 1, 1799 Isaac sold part of the 450 acres to Elias with, *"a griss mill and saw mill house."* Sylvia wrote in her report: *"In 1841 Elias Conklin sold some of his property to his nephews Isaac and John D. Conklin, sons of his brother Isaac. Isaac paid $200 for 99 acres which included the house in which Elias then lived, which is the one now occupied by Mr. and Mrs. Van Smith. In 1846 Elias sold the grist mill to his grand-nephew, Reuben son of John D. Conklin, for $350. Reuben died in 1854 and the mill was awarded to his brothers, Milton, Daniel and Jacob."* It appears that Daniel built the house on the opposite side of the creek near the mill about 1855. J. Milton Conklin lived in it for about twenty years before his death.

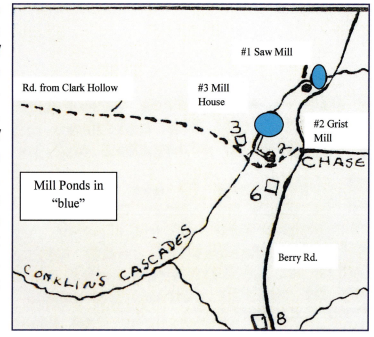

John D. Conklin likely built the house on the northeast corner of Chase and Berry Roads about the time that he acquired the land from his uncle (now 6707 Chase Rd.) He had previously lived farther south along Berry Rd. next to his cousin, Josiah D., but that house disappeared between the maps of 1860 and 1874. Of John D.'s and Sally Hanchett's six children only one married. He was the youngest, Daniel, but he had no surviving children. After Reuben died, the remaining four, Fanny, Fidelia, Jacob and John Milton, lived together in John D.'s house where he died in 1866. Although J. Milton was the youngest of these four he was always listed in the census as the "head of house-hold".

"Pompey -...Two more sudden deaths have occurred in the community, the first was that of Isaac Conklin, an aged man living near Conklin's Mill. He had been ailing for several days but feeling better, he performed his usual duties on Monday the 3rd. In the evening he rose from his bed where he had been resting and in making his way back again, fell dead..." (Syracuse Journal, Feb. 19, 1879) And two years later, Jacob Conklin died. *"Pompey – The angel of death has been hovering over these beautiful hills for a time and again we are called to notice the house of mourning. This time the one taken from near our border in LaFayette was Jacob Conklin, in the full vigor of manhood, Friday last [Oct. 21] after a painful illness of only a few days..." (Note: One of the Conklin brothers – aged 57) (Syracuse Courier, Oct. 26, 1881)* The last surviving sibling was Fanny, who was living in February, 1892 but died later that year at the age of 74. From then on Milton lived alone near the mill except for a house keeper. In 1900 she was Miss Florence Stanton, sister of a well-known photographer, Henry Stanton, who took several superb photographs of Milton, his mill and the falls.

After selling the house to Isaac Jr. as cited above, Elias Conklin went to live with his daughter, Betsey, and her husband Warner Butts (No. 6). They lived across from what is now the west entrance to Berwyn Cemetery. There he died in 1854 and there also his grandson, Heber Butts, lived in 1875 when the unfortunate incident occurred mentioned at page 62.

It is enough to say that a declining and insufficient amount of water rendered the mill dormant during the summer months. To recover this deficiency, J. Milton and Jacob purchased a steam engine in 1874. *"Pompey...Conklin Bros., who live just across the line in LaFayette but are virtually identified with us in all our business and social interests, have just put a new steam engine into their excellent flouring mill and propose hereafter to promptly accommodate their line of work. Their marked integrity and uprightness in business and their excellent flour, equal to the best in the country, cannot fail to bring them increased patronage and prosperity. They have the best wishes of the community that their enterprise may be abundantly rewarded." (Syracuse Journal, Nov. 6, 1874)* The cost of the steam engine was prohibitive and they went bankrupt. The Pompey Hill "Courier" correspondent reported on April 29, 1881: *"The failure of the Messrs. Conklin, of LaFayette, is seriously felt in Pompey. Their creditors here are quite numerous, in sums ranging from one to three and four hundred dollars. No one can yet tell what percentage they can pay."* A week later the correspondent brought an up-date: *"Mr. Miller, assignee of the Conklin brothers, thinks their assets will pay about 75 per cent of their indebtedness."* The mill was never again self-sufficient. When Morris Beard of Pompey died in 1904 he left the mortgage on the property, which he had held for many years, to the Pompey Disciples Church. Still nothing could be paid on it by the aged J. Milton and in 1911 it was foreclosed; he went to the County Poor House where he died in December, 1913 aged 86. After standing vacant for another decade the old mill was torn down for salvage by Elton Downing assisted by his older sons in 1923.

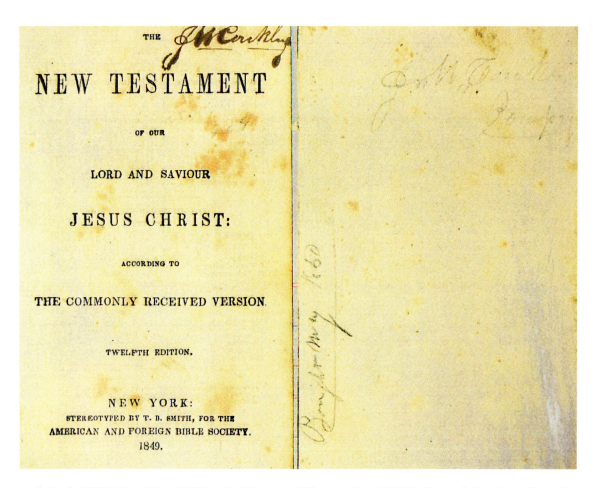

Fly leaf of "J.M. Conkling's" Bible which he noted "Bought May, 1850". He used the old spelling of the name which also appears on the deeds of 1797 and 1799.

John Milton Conklin standing in the roadway leading down to his mill in the distance. It is said that Jirah D. Palmer would not grind buckwheat at his modern turbine powered Collingwood Mills but referred it to Mr. Conklin so that the old man would have some small means of support.

"...Today all there is left of the Conklin business is the old mill building with the roof full of holes, the walls crumbling and the timbers decaying and a small fraction of the machinery. The old engine and boiler are gone, every little piece of brass, copper or cast iron that any Jew junk dealer could steal is gone, the gears and belting have disappeared. The building is sold to be torn down and drawn away. One can read in these old ruins the history of men and nations as well as of industries; each has its period of growth and glory and decay..." (Milton Downing, 1921)

"John Milton Conklin, 86, supervisor of the town of LaFayette in the years of 1865-66, died at the County Hospital. He was born on the farm near Berwin where he spent his life as a farmer and miller. His father owned a large farm and at his death he left it to his two sons and two daughters, none of whom ever married; the last of John Milton's brothers and sisters died fifteen years ago leaving him alone. He ran the grist mill which his grandfather had built over a hundred years ago, until three years ago." ("Tully Times", Dec. 11, 1913)

"John Milton Conklin, 86, died at the County hospital Sunday afternoon (Dec. 7) where he had been a patient for about a week. He leaves no relatives." (Fayetteville "Recorder", Dec. 12, 1913)

When Morris Beard died in 1904 he left the mortgage on this property to the Pompey Disciples Church. In 1911 the church foreclosed it. In 1919 the mill and mill house on about four acres were sold to Albert Carley for $450.

In 1923 the mill was taken down by Elton Downing and sons. Eventually the site came into possession of Richard N. Wright whose family used the house as a summer camp, lastly in 1941. Wright sold it to Ollie Sheremeta, City Editor of the Syracuse "Post-Standard", and a resident of Clark Hollow Rd., LaFayette.

IN PURSUANCE OF AN ORDER MADE by the Hon. H. Riegel, County Judge of Onondaga County, on the 28th day of June, 1881, notice is hereby given to all the creditors and persons having claims against Jacob Conklin and John M. Conklin, lately doing business in the town of LaFayette, and County of Onondaga, under the firm name of J.M. Conklin & Brother, that they are required to present their claims with the vouchers therefore, duly verified, to the subscriber, the duly appointed assignee of the said Jacob Conklin and John M. Conklin, and firm of J.M. Conklin & Brother, for the benefit of their creditors, at his dwelling house in the town of LaFayette, on or before the 15th day of September, 1881. Dated June 28, 1881.

MAUS V. MILLER, Assignee.
Postoffice address, Pompey.

LANSING & LYMAN, Attys for Assignee.

(Syracuse Journal, June 28, 1881)

ASSIGNEE'S SALE — A STEAM AND water power Flouring Mill, dwelling house and two acres of land, located in LaFayette, Onondaga county, N.Y., lately owned by J.M. Conklin & Bro., are offered for sale. A great bargain will be given. Address, MAUS V. MILLER, Assignee, Pompey, Onondaga Co., N.Y.

(Syracuse Journal, June 28, 1881)
(Syracuse Journal, July 2, 1881)

"Clarence White has sold the land around Conklin's Falls, as well as the falls, to Mr. and Mrs. Robert Colvin from Syracuse.

(Tully Independent, Sept. 13, 1957)

J. Milton Conklin seated with some of his cats. "The ceaseless grinding of the stones, creaking of the wheel, and noise of pulleys, belting and gears had deafened the ancient miller. Like vanished echoes of the past the noise took on its own meaning, and a multitude of cats were his only companions. A resident of Berwyn came to the mill to buy some bran. In the midst of filling the order, the old man spied one of his favorite cats and carefully articulated over the noise of the mill, 'Kitty! Kitty! Are you the kitty that shit in the bran?'

(LaFayette, NY: A History, 1975, pg. 148)

"...One by one the Conklins died. Reuben who had purchased the mill from his uncle Elias was first. That was in 1854 aged 31, before his parents. Daniel, the only one of the brothers to marry but he had no children, died in 1872 aged 42. Jacob, who listed himself as carpenter on certain census, died in 1881 aged 57. Maiden sisters Fanny and Fidelia went in their middle 70's, the last being Fanny in 1892.

    John Milton, a graduate of Hamilton College where he is said to have studied the classics, was the sole survivor by nearly twenty years. Local boys who crept up to his dimly lit window watched him read and believed it was his Latin and Greek. When visiting the mill they remembered him quoting the ancient poets. After his death his worn possessions were held up to view at auction and there were some of the texts..."   (<u>LaFayette, N.Y.: A History</u> *(1975) J. Roy Dodge)*

Notice the penstock which carried water to the overshot wheel in each of the above photos.

End view of three-story Conklin grist mill with addition which housed the steam engine.

Sylvia Shoebridge salvaged two of the Conklin millstones and took this photo in 1978. Writing in 1980 for her tour of "Conklin Mills and Settlement" by the Pompey Historical Society she noted: "The millstones are made from New York State conglomerate stone which is found in the Shawngunk area – just below the Catskill mountains.

The millstones measure 51 inches across and 12 inches deep."

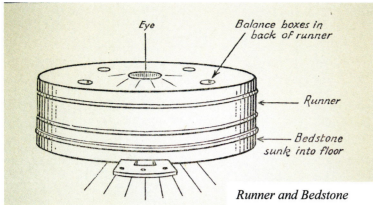

Runner and Bedstone

Millstones come in pairs. The base or bedstone is stationary. Above the bedstone is the turning runner stone which actually does the grinding. The runner stone spins above the stationary bedstone creating a "scissoring" or grinding action of the stones.

View of the penstock from the corner of the mill

Mill pond with water inlet to the Conklin millrace.

Mill race bringing water from mill pond to penstock. Note presence of man standing on bank at right,

May, 1902

Drawing of an overshot mill wheel which was said to offer 75% water efficiency.

"At the Mill Dam"

by E.Q. Williams, 1890

Looking toward the mill dam at high water.

The bulkheads of the dam were washed out in March, 1884,

adding to John Milton Conklin's financial difficulties.

The mill dam at low water, 1877 (Stereo view)

Then and Now: Where the mill dam stood as photographed in July, 1980

CONKLIN'S FALLS

*Two young couples of Berwyn had their picture taken near Mr. Conklin's smoke house
by Henry Stanton, 1902 or '03.*
Left to right: Chessie Daley (d. 1923 as the first wife of Arthur Morrison); Arthur Morrison (1885-1953); Jessie Haviland (1884-1976); Homer Newcomb (1882-1965). Jessie and Homer married later.

It seems likely that some of those who will read these lines have never heard of Conklin's Falls and even fewer have seen them. But in the 19th century they were well-known, their sylvan setting and bucolic charm idyllic to those who tramped over rugged terrain to view them. Very early in photography their image was a popular attraction and we have several in the collection; stereo views from 1877 and four shots by E.Q. Williams in 1890. Later, when photographic equipment was less cumbersome, many more outings were recorded by the camera. French's Gazetteer of the State of New York (1860) notes that the water falls 500 feet in less than a mile on Conklin's Brook.

And it was not just local adolescents with strong stamina who braved the rugged paths. On June 27, 1877, "*a large party of ladies and gentlemen including ex-Senator Wood and Daniel Gott Esq. passed through Pompey on a pic-nic excursion to Conklin's Falls three miles south of us,"* recorded Luella Dunham in the "Journal" of six days later. *"We do not wonder that former residents of Pompey enjoy such excursions and bring their friends with them to revisit memory dear."* These former Pompey worthies, sons of prominent fathers of the same name, were no "spring chickens" when this visit was made.

"Pompey – The picnic that was to be held at Conklin's Falls on Tues. was postponed until Wed. afternoon on account of the rain. The afternoon was fine and the pleasure seekers enjoyed themselves immensely. They all returned to their respective homes well satisfied with their visit to the falls." (Syracuse Standard, Aug. 8, 1878)

A 1912 newspaper article about Berwyn mentioned a *"Mrs. Hart of Geneva and Miss Berk Hart of Syracuse recently spent a few days at James Partridge's. Mrs. Hart who is 70 years young made a trip to Conklin's Falls with apparent ease over a route that tries the physical powers of many people much younger. A party of young people returning from the falls a few days ago called on Mr. Milton Conklin the venerable old gentleman who for many years has operated the famous Conklin's Mills and were pleasantly entertained by that gentleman who gave them information of interest regarding the falls and the early history of Berwyn. Mr. Conklin is a graduate of Hamilton College and is the possessor of a splendid library."* (T.T., ca.1912)

Homer Newcomb on J. M. Conklin's smoke house, privy in back. Photo by Henry Stanton

On June 18, 1933 the Syracuse Post-Standard featured a story on Berwyn in its "Forgotten Villages" series. Robert C. Hill of that early LaFayette family wrote some further recollections in a letter to the editor. "A brief description of this hinterland called Marionville, afterward Berwyn may be of interest to you, if not the waste basket is handy. Three miles northeast of Apulia Station is a section of the country called Berwyn. Seventy years ago the post office went by the name of Marionville. When rural free delivery came along the post office was abandoned. Now it is a difficult matter to find just where Marionville stood. Until recently this section was indeed a hinterland, but now the CWA forces are working on the road and the inhabitants, or rather natives, are getting over their shyness and will often talk to the passing traveler. Near Berwyn stood Conklin's mill, one of the first mills erected in this locality. It was torn down a few years ago after the death of Milton Conklin who was the last of the Conklins, I believe, and a graduate of Hamilton College.

The writer remembers the mill, located in a romantic glen. There was a water wheel 30 feet in diameter; also an auxiliary steam plant. (Note: most sources agree that the overshot water wheel was 24 feet in diameter.) Fifty years ago the mill was in fair repair, but the business had dwindled to farmers' grist. It is said that at one time large quantities of buckwheat came to the mill as it was equipped with the best machines for grinding and preparing pancake flour.

Not far from the mill site is the home of the Cooks. Seward Cook had the first steam threshing machine in town. Delos Cook, his son, ran the engine for many years as a boy and man, and afterward had threshing rigs of his own. The old steam engine still stands back of the house, and around the premises may be seen the remains of sawmills, tractors, threshers and farm machinery representing an investment of many thousands of dollars. Somewhere in this locality is the "Woodford district", once the home of the Woodfords, a prolific and representative old American family, now, alas, few in number. Israel Woodford drove the mail stage from Pompey to LaFayette.

I believe an interesting article could be made of Berwyn and its inhabitants. Of course it would be well to wait until the roses bloom again before venturing into these wilds. In the spring, when warm weather comes, the natives get their hair cuts and nature will be grand to take photos. Conklin Falls are not far away and well worth the trouble getting to them and Berwyn is unique." (Post Standard, June 27, 1933)

MISS DUNHAM'S VISIT TO CONKLIN'S FALLS --- 1879

NOTE: Luella Sophia Dunham was an unmarried lady of 28 when she wrote this story for publication in the Fayetteville "Weekly Recorder' on July 15, 1879. She was the Pompey Hill correspondent to that paper beginning June 15, 1872. In those days most of the local correspondents to various newspapers adopted a pen name; Luella's was "Alpha". The Pompey Hill correspondent to the "Syracuse Journal" wrote under the name "Scribe" but in the spring of 1876 he decided to "Go West" and on

March 28, 1876 she sent a letter to the "Journal" which she noted in her scrapbook as "first letter to the Journal as regular correspondent". She chose the nom de plume "Gleaner" and later used that for the "Recorder' as well. Her output started small; only nine letters to the "Recorder" in 1873. But at her peak in 1879 when this story was submitted she tallied up her production at the end of the year as 46 which she noted as "Standard 1, Courier 1, Journal 20, Recorder 22 aside from talks about Pompey Hill." She was being a bit too modest for her 'talks about Pompey Hill' was a veritable history of every building, business and early personality in that place. Luella continued to write until her last submission in 1884. After a lingering illness, she died on July 8, 1886 at the age of 35.

In front of the second falls after a summer freshet in July, 1900.
Emily Haviland (Mrs. Will), Florence M. Stanton, Will Haviland, perhaps Mrs. Henry Stanton seated.

"ONE MORNING IN JUNE"

"Some friends called for me one fine June morning to go with them to Conklin's Falls and I, equally pleased with their kind thoughtfulness and the prospects in view, readily assented. We were soon bounding over the road drawn by those superb horses. If some of the guests that were in town last year could have seen this fine span, I am sure that they would have been less ready to make sport of Pompey horseflesh. The team is superior to any hereabouts. I always stop to admire them when they are in sight, grand and beautiful in their superior proportions. The morning was clear, bright, breezy and bracing, the landscape far-spread in extent. Every point of the glorious exhibition of vegetation showed to advantage in the crystalline atmosphere. Before fairly leaving the village, the sublime hill scenery at the south and west, diversified with deep graceful depressions, crowned with matchless woodlands and veined with delightful ravines, began to make itself felt and with all the grandeur and loveliness combined, aroused every perception with a thrill of ecstasy, and seemed to fill heart and soul with exuberant exhilaration. On we rode, discussing the families, farmhouses and crops.

We entered the Woodford neighborhood, now Marionville post office, whose official name was bestowed less than a year ago, but we do not traverse the thickest settled portion, but on coming to a fork in the road, we kept to the right instead of up the rise, through an avenue of maples. (This is where Berwyn and Collins Rds., now so called, diverge).

We turned just by the cheese factory. Had we kept on the same road, instead, less than a mile would have brought us to the border line between Fabius and Pompey. (Here Luella turned right into Chase Rd. The cheese factory was on the southeast corner of Chase and Collins Rds. It was built by Ansel Woodford in May, 1874 and burned March 12, 1881. It was never replaced.) A few rods to the westward brought us into the town of LaFayette. Wild wayside growths on either hand were most luxuriant; the reedy cattail, a miniature wilderness of June roses loaded with delicate gems, blackberries laden with blossoming pearls, and a tiny blue water-plant were fine studies for the artist's eye. At the south, and surrounded by fields, is the neighborhood burial ground.

Arriving at the cross-roads, we turned neither to the right nor the left, but kept on down the steep hill to the mill. (Here she crossed present Berry Rd.) On the right is a precipitous wooded bank reaching to the edge of the creek and the picturesque milldam; at the left is a towering bank high above our heads. The grist would not be ready in an hour, and leaving the horses, we proceeded on foot toward the falls, following the meanders of the stream, here crossing on the stones that rise above the water and farther on leaping the splashy places with all the ease and grace that narrow skirts and pull-backs will allow. Now, pausing to admire lichens on some decaying log, then watching the reflection of rippling water on the smooth worn side of an ancient stump.

The green-jacketed and white-vested frogs gave us a fine concert, each striving to outdo the other. Funny frog stories were told; the best was that about a man who, after long consideration, finally concluded to set out selling brooms. After he had fairly started on his trip, he sat down near a stream to rest and his interpretation of what the frogs were saying was in this wise: "Eaton! – Eaton! – Selling brooms? Selling brooms? -- Better go home. Better go home.", which advice he immediately acted upon. The pathway by the side of the brook is hemmed in by hills. On the west rises a steep wooded height that will soon be bare and desolate, if the axe is allowed to despoil the forest more. On the east and at the front rises a high hill. The driveway into the wood is from the road above through a field, now forbidden to public use by the present proprietor, Mr. Fitzgerald, unless an admittance fee of twenty-five cents is paid which will enable him to hire a boy to put up the bars after the careless visitor who usually leaves them down, letting in cattle that raise a riot with the grain.

One of the finest stereoscopic views that has been photographed in this region is from that high point, embracing the hills on both sides and the brook between; trees, stumps and logs, the winding highway from whence our footsteps came, a woodland yet higher up, a glimpse of the red mill and the white dwelling near, forming a picture worthy a production in oil by an eminent painter.

Full view of the second falls after a summer freshet, July 1900. Photo by Henry Stanton.

Crossing the rustic stile, we were fairly in the woods. It was difficult picking a pathway, thrusting through the clinging underbrush as it grew wilder and more uncouth with rude natural obstacles, plunging this way, now that, to find a way less obstructed, pausing again to admire a beautiful young hemlock and the dense growth of ferns at its feet, sniffing the aromatic fragrance of both, discussing the beauty of the profuse wild geranium, peering into a black sullen pool, mournful to a surpassing degree, we emerged at the top of the upper falls. After viewing the little that can be seen of the cascade from that point, we followed the wild well-trodden path along the top of the high bank, and down that peculiar, almost perpendicular steep between two precipices, wide at the top and narrowing downward to a mere point. We clambered down the beetling crag as best we could, over a soft carpet of dead hemlock leaves and decayed wood, making careful footholds in the fantastically twisted tree roots that lie bare in the way, and finally seated ourselves at the point of declivity at the top of the second fall. We looked back with wonder at the angle down which we had come. Nature sometimes secretes her hidden beauties in a manner impossible for humanity to penetrate, but in a generous mood she fitted this wonderful path that we might have a desirable communion seat and a way whereby to reach the foot of the upper fall.

The second falls with almost no water flowing, 1915.

I find it a difficult task to paint an accurate word picture of Conklin's Falls, so largely does the mysterious wildwood enter into the scene and affect the views of the three distinct and successive cascades. They would perhaps average eighty feet each in height and some sixty rods distant from each other. They are varied, not perpendicular but continually broken, so that the beauty is enhanced certainly tenfold. The first fall is the prettiest of the three, the second even more wild, and those undertaking to secure full views of the second and third must encounter almost break-neck difficulties. Encompassed as they are by a dense forest, it gives a weird, somber air and render them exceedingly grand, but to analyze the characteristic beauties of the cascades irrespective of surroundings, they are smiling, lovely, charming and highly picturesque, lacking the grandeur, the majesty, and failing to inspire the thrill of grateful thanksgiving that fills the heart of the beholder at Pratt's Falls. Notwithstanding Conklin's is the favorite with almost everyone, my preference is entirely for Pratt's.

We linger and still linger, unmindful of the voice that bids us 'Come'. We climb the ascent in a manner that made it seem reasonable man had from his remote ancestor quadruped as Mr. Darwin asserts. When at the top, we stooped to pluck the partridge berries that offered themselves at our feet, the growth of last autumn but ripened only in the spring time, and now red as drops of blood, and were well pleased with their wild flavor. Lingering beside a tree trunk which some blast overthrew long ago, and which time ever since had been covering with moss, a partridge whirred away from its nest in a decaying stump. The voice still bade us 'Come'.

The grist was not ready on our return to the mill so we wandered to the pretty cascade formed by the dam, with a tranquil mirror lake at its base, and seeking out a back-log, engaged in confidential chat until it was time to go. Reaching the cross-roads at the top of the steep, we turned to the left returning home by another route. I have inquired in vain for any noteworthy landmarks or traditions on our way toward the State road. The smiling landscape afforded studies in the varied green of the forest trees in their wealth of early summer foliage. The village (LaFayette) cresting the northwest is occasionally seen over the tree-tops. Finally we emerge upon the State road, catching a charming view of Jamesville, seemingly nestled by the blue waters of the reservoir, the darker blue of the wild landscape northward making a fine background…"

Syracuse photographer John Winter managed to get his equipment to this spot just below the foot of the falls in the second half of the 1890's.
The people are not identified nor how they were able to walk up the creek dressed as they are.

WOMAN A SUICIDE.
Miss Mary Ann Morrison's Body Found in Mill Pond

"The body of Miss Mary Ann Morrison, recently a patient at the Hospital for Women and Children, was found yesterday in the Conklin mill pond, half a mile below Conklin Falls, near the junction of the Lafayette, Pompey and Fabius town lines. Miss Morrison evidently went straight from the home of her aunt, Mrs. James Partridge at Lafayette, to the pond. The little daughter of Albert Sherman reported to her mother that she saw a bundle of woman's clothing in the water. Mrs. Sherman investigated and called Augustus Krakeau, who got the body out of the water. Miss Morrison, who was 61 years old, was subject to melancholia. She has two sisters in this city. Coroner Willer investigated the case and gave a verdict of suicide." *(The Syracuse Herald, Sat. Evening, 10 July 1909)*

FAY – Drowned, in Pompey, about 2 ½ miles southwest of Pompey Hill, in Conklin's mill pond, Howard C., son of Paul Fay, and grandson of Vliet Carpenter, of DeWitt, on Tuesday the 14th, between 4 and 5 o'clock PM, aged 12 years, 6 months and 14 days. Funeral services at the house at 11 ½ o'clock Sunday, the 19th. *(The Syracuse Journal, June 17, 1870)*

DODGE-BUSH RE-UNION, 1922

The Dodge-Bush Reunions were held on the Roy Dodge farm, Clark Hollow Rd. through the 1920's. He is seated on the ground in the front row.

Much more activity was evident at the Conklin falls according to other newspaper articles. "The Bush Reunion was held at Conklin Falls Sunday." *(T.T., Thurs., 9 Aug 1928)*.

The "Apulia M.E. Church will hold the annual picnic for the Sunday School at Conklin Falls on Thursday, July 11th. Drive to the residence of Elton Downing and you will be shown the rest of the way." *(Tully Times, Thurs., July 4, 1929).*

Sunday School Picnic, 1927

Onativia Sunday School Picnic, 1927
Irvin Hughes, Pearle Weller, Belle Weller

In 1936, "the LaFayette High school students and faculty enjoyed a wiener roast at Conklin Falls Thursday evening." *(T.T., Thurs., 13 June 1936)*. The "LaFayette Boy Scouts spent the weekend at Conklin Falls." *(T.T., Thurs., 20 Nov 1947)*. The "Boy Scout committee members are soliciting funds for the boys' camp at Conklin Falls." *(T.T., Thurs., 13 Sep 1947)*.

"Sunday, being as it was, friends and us were out in the country south of the Cherry Valley Turnpike. We parked and hiked back in the woods along a stream until we came to the Conklin Falls. The brook and falls attract many during the summer picnic time and it is also the camping site of Troop 100, LaFayette Boy Scouts, who have a small rustic cabin, back in. Along this brook and the Butternut, which we crossed going and coming, the willows are starting to turn red. Ah, Spring!" (Syracuse Herald Journal, CITY LIFE *by Joe Beamish, Wed., 6 Feb. 1952.)*

First or Lower Falls, 1890

Conklin's Second Fall, Side View by E.Q. Williams, 1890

Conklin's 2nd Falls, Front View by E.Q. Williams, 1890

BEAUTY SPOT AT DOORSTEP OF SYRACUSE
CASCADE FALLS DROPS 250 FEET
HIDDEN FROM VIEW
Few Residents of Central New York Aware of Scenic Wonder

"Movement to convert Cascade Falls Valley in the town of LaFayette into a New York State Park has been launched by residents of LaFayette, Pompey, Tully and Fabius. Harry J. Clark, secretary of Onondaga County Parks and Planning Commission and Michael G. Shea, supervisor of the Town of Fabius, one of the leaders of the project, will visit the falls this week to investigate the feasibility of improving the area and throwing it open to the public as one of the chain of State parks in Central New York.

Here, within 15 miles of the heart of Syracuse, one of the most beautiful waterfalls in the entire State is so well hidden from view that it is improbable that more than one in a hundred in Onondaga County knows of its existence. Even Supervisor Shea, who has lived in Fabius less than four miles from the falls for more than fifty years, never saw the cascades until this week.

Pouring out of a series of springs in the southwestern part of the Town of Pompey, a stream of pure clear water flows southwesterly into the Town of LaFayette, where it tumbles over four cascades, an aggregate drop of 250 feet with one-eighth of a mile. The three lower cascades presents one view, one of the most beautiful scenic displays in the East, the water as

Stereo photo – probably 1877

it tumbles over the rocky ledges, being churned to snow white foam.

The upper cascade, hidden by a bend in the stream, is well worth a climb up the rock-walled chasm, for 200 feet above its three sister cascades, it shoots down 80 feet, a great sheet of water. For a quarter mile below the falls the stream flows through a canyon with walls more than 100 feet high. Then the valley widens and the creek finally emerges into pasture land and joins a stream flowing down the Jamesville-Apulia Valley.

Proponents of the State Park project point out that it would be comparatively easy to clear the bushes and undergrowth from the wider part of the valley, and that walks and paths could be constructed through the heavy woods that cover the steep slopes near the cascades. Entrance to the Cascades is effected from the dirt road leading from Apulia to the Pompey-Onativia highway.

About a mile south of what will be a link in the Cherry Valley Turnpike extending across the State and a great artery of traffic, is an old barn and a cellar over which a house once stood. A colony of bees is the only sign of life. This little farmyard, sponsors of the park idea say, could be obtained at a reasonable figure and would lend itself admirably to a park entrance and parking place for automobiles. One hundred rods from the road the visitor picks up the stream as it winds down through a cow pasture.

Following the course of the creek he soon finds himself in a narrow gully with rocky walls back of which are thickly wooded hills. Working his way onward and upward through thick underbrush and climbing over or crawling under fallen trees, at the end of a quarter mile he is greeted by the sight of the queen of Central New York waterfalls.

Residents of southern Onondaga County interested in the development of this natural beauty spot point out that the State has spent great sums of money in building parks with far less beautiful features. Even Watkins Glen, far famed wonder of the Southern Tier which is visited by a half million or more tourists each year, is not so much more beautiful or attractive that Cascade Falls Valley.

Thousands of Syracusans and residents of other sections of the State annually visit such scenic beauty spots as Chittenango Falls, Edwards Falls, Triphammer Falls and others as widely known. But none of them surpass, and few of them equal in beauty, this series of cascades in the Town of LaFayette only 20 minutes drive from Clinton Square. They are a scenic wonder at the doorstep of Syracuse which the great majority of its residents know nothing. While the charms of other natural beauties have been widely broadcast, the peer of any of them had been unheralded and unsung.

If Supervisor Shea and his supporters in the State park project have their way, Cascade Falls is about to come into its own." *(Syracuse "Herald", October 20, 1929).*

During the 1930's rumors carried the news that the falls would be developed as a park. Then and later the problem was always the same; the remote location and the number of owners involved in the property. On the lower or Clark Hollow end, Leroy Dodge had acquired, about 1890, what was called the Dean farm with a house and barn upon it and extending to the base of the falls. The unoccupied house soon fell down but as the barn was useful for hay storage it stood into the 1980's. In 1964 the property was sold by Dodge's grandson, Guy, to William G. Moench who owned it about thirty years. A new house has since been built on the site of the old one by Keith and Ann Wickes in 1990.

"Sold to LeRoy Dodge About 1890"
Barn which stood north of what is now 1864 Clark Hollow Rd., driveway at center leading to the foot of Conklin's Falls. House was at right.

Lot #91 Owners: - 1852, J. Butts; 1874 & 1889, A. Dean. Sold to LeRoy Dodge about 1900, then to his grandson Guy Dodge who sold it about 1964 to Wm. Moench. Barn fell down 1980's.

In possible preparation of the park project, Onondaga County began bridge repair in Berwyn in the autumn of 1959. "The county has improved the bridge near Conklin Falls, but spoiled the old swimming hole for the old as well as the young who enjoyed a nice dip when the weather was hot." *(Tully Independent, Thurs., Aug. 3, 1959) It had been known as the "Berwyn bath tub".*

Bridge on Berry Road, LaFayette over Conklin's Creek.

PARK BOARD TO BUY LAND IN LAFAYETTE

"The Onondaga County Park Board is in the process of purchasing 150 to 200 acres in the Cascades area of the Town of LaFayette. Work of obtaining options on this property is slated to begin shortly. The Parks Board is in the process of buying nearly 1,200 acres of Onondaga County land to make sure future generations will have recreational facilities. Efforts are being made to take necessary steps before Jan. 1. State funds will be used in buying the land options; descriptions and appraisals are all involved in the work of the Board in directing its program." *("Tully Independent", October 19, 1961)*

LAFAYETTE RANKS AS THIRD CHOICE
FOR FUTURE COUNTY PARK SITE

"An area in LaFayette is currently ranking third for possible development into a county park, according to the Onondaga County Public Works Commissioner for Parks & Recreation.

The area being considered is south of Route 20 and has been set aside as Cascade Park. The County does not have an option to buy the land, an area of 150 to 200 acres and owned by several persons. Other sites being considered is Beaver Lake, also known as Mud Lake in the Town of Lysander, and two sites in the Town of Cicero." *("Tully Independent", August 2, 1962)*

At the time the Commissioner noted that, *"the County does not have an option to buy the land owned by several persons."* That was the end of the idea, probably forever. In the meantime, the pasture and open fields described by Luella Dunham have been reclaimed by nature and now every foot of it is a forest almost as deep as the primeval one first viewed by the Conklin brothers.

View along Conklin Creek by Henry Stanton early 1900's. All of it is now reclaimed by nature.

Another winter view along Conklin Creek by Henry Stanton early 1900's. This and the scenes on pages 43 and 53 were also printed as post cards.

TOUR OPENS UP THE OLD MILL STREAM

by ROBERT L. SMITH of *The Post-Standard, July 14, 1994*

"THE VIEW from Berry Road at the southern edge of Pompey is one to forget. A sluggish brown stream slides into a dark, weedy wood and disappears. Most motorists breeze by without a thought. Too bad, because just inside, a story explodes in natural beauty. That distant roar is Conklin Creek, spilling over one, then two, then three spectacular cascades on a rush to Butternut Creek, through a glen steeped in history. Wednesday, people will be welcomed into the privately owned valley for a rare glimpse into the area's past. The Pompey Historical Society is sponsoring a tour of the Conklin Cascades and the remains of two mills — one for wood and one for flour — that once harnessed the creek's power. The curious should report to Chase Road near Berry Road in LaFayette at 7 p.m. Pompey town historian Sylvia Shoebridge will lead the tour. Be prepared for details.

Shoebridge's interest in the Conklin mills runs from fascination to personal. Her maiden name is Berry, and she lives just up Berry Road, in the farmhouse her family built in 1808. They would have arrived about the same time as Elias Conklin. - Conklin's grist mill — which operated for more than 100 years, Shoebridge said. And early mills anywhere tell a tale of rugged pioneers. "The first thing you built was a saw mill, so people could build houses," she said. "Then they had to grind grain for bread." Shoebridge spent 14 years researching the two mill sites and then secured the permission of two property owners for a one-time tour. Her information will flesh out a lot of what people can no longer see. Time and the power of the creek erased most of what was once a mighty millworks in a thriving little settlement. The grist mill, for example, rose three stories high. It closed in 1913, and only low ruins remain. The Conklin house, also built in 1808, still stands on Chase Road above the stream.

The historical record fills in the rest of the story. New York opened up the area in 1790, offering tracts of land to Revolutionary War veterans. Most of the early settlers, like the Berry family, came from Connecticut, built log and then wood-frame houses, and farmed the land. Conklin had his mill running by at least 1798, when a survey tells of a road leading to it. Shoebridge said she believes the floorboards in her house were sawed at Conklin's mill. "There were mills all over Pompey", Shoebridge said. "But there's no other mill site that has so much information. That's why this one is so interesting. It's a link to our past."

"Fishing on Conklin's Creek"

Photograph taken by Henry Stanton about 1901, west and downstream of Conklin's mill. Florence Stanton at left and Carl, one of the Swift twins, fishing in front of unknown woman. Miss Stanton called the house visible above the creek "Brookside".

"Two of the 'boys from Berwyn', Rev. Carl C. Swift and Mr. and Mrs. Gerald Frost returned to the scenes of their childhood last Saturday. They visited Conklin Falls after the passage of nearly 60 years and enjoyed reminiscences of the Sunday school picnics and group outings that used to be held at that well beloved spot. They also recounted their memories of the wonderful Conklin's mill and J. Milton Conklin, the last of his race, whose story of devotion to the family mill makes the stuff of history, if not of fiction. They are 76 and 77 years of age, yet they walked up the creek to the falls as nimble as teenagers." (Tully Independent, Aug. 15, 1974)

Along the Creek

Looking north to the Morrison farm, now Elliott's at 2117 Berry Rd.

The line of a worked field south of the buildings is the line of town lots 77 & 92. Ansel Woodford (1817-1904) owned the farm of 108 acres c. 1854 to c. 1870. Then it was sold to his son-in-law James Morrison with his wife, Delia, and nine children. James was born in England and came to America when he was ten years old. He grew up on a farm along Swift Rd. now site of the Pompey Rod & Gun Club. He died of an apparent heart attack May 22, 1885. He was 46 years old. Property in the foreground, left side of the road, is part of John D. Conklin's "100 acres" purchased from his uncle, Elias Conklin, in 1841.

Haying on Jim Morrison farm at Berry Road c. 1901 or '02.

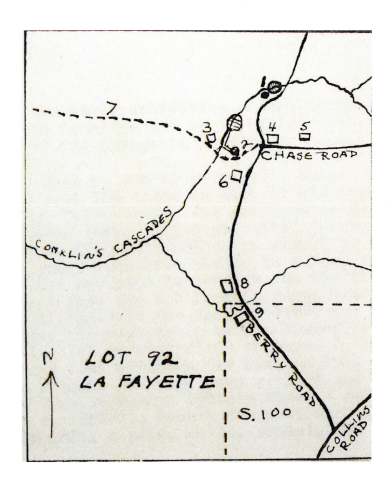

SYLVIA SHOEBRIDGE'S CONKLIN MAP, 1978

1. Conklin saw mill and mill pond, later rebuilt by James Partridge.
2. Conklin grist and flour mill and mill pond.
3. House probably built by Daniel Conklin about 1855. It was later occupied by John Milton Conklin for many years.
4. House built by John D. Conklin, later occupied by his maiden daughters Fanny and Fidelia. John D. was also the father of J. Milton, Reuben, Daniel and Jacob.
5. This was the original home of Elias Conklin which he sold to his nephew, Isaac, in 1841.
6. Elias Conklin built this house for his son-in-law, Warren Butts, and here he died in 1854.
7. Road laid out in 1800 from the mill to Sherman Hollow for the convenience of getting to Conklin's. It was last used about 1912 when the mill ceased operation. It was known as "Miner Hill"
8. & 9. Josiah D. Conklin (1812-1886), son of Elias had two houses here. Number 9 is still standing

House (No. 4) built by John D. Conklin on 100 acres he purchased from his uncle, Elias, in 1841. The unmarried brothers and sisters lived here until about 1892 when the property was sold. This picture was taken in June, 1933 for the "Post-Standard" series "Forgotten Villages". Now 6707 Chase Rd.

No. 4 – The early activities of the Conklins are noted in "The Conklins and their Mills" from the newsletter of the LaFayette Historical Society of April, 2008.

In 1841, when he was 67 years old, Elias Conklin(1774-1854) sold 100 acres to each of his nephews on the same day. This portion was conveyed to John D. Conklin. John D. Conklin (Dec.1787-Sep.1866) married Sally Hanchett (Nov.1794-July1856). An effort to connect her to the other Hanchetts living in Pompey at an early date has not been successful. On the Census of 1855 she said that she was born in Pennsylvania and her son J. Milton said the same in 1900. She was received into the membership of the Pompey Congregational Church (called Presbyterian) on Sep. 5, 1823. She presented her five children for baptism Feb. 13, 1828. They were: Frances Melitta, born c. 1818 and known throughout her life as Fanny; Cynthia Fidelia born c. 1820; Jacob born c. 1822/23; Reuben Hanchett born 1824; John Milton born 1827. A sixth child, Daniel, was born 1830.

The deed of April 15, 1841 conveying 100 acres to John D. included, "all the ground now used and occupied by the saw mill, saw mill pond, and mill yard and all that may be necessary for the keeping of the said mill and dam in repair forever – excepting also so much of said premises as is flowed by the grist mill pond…" In a separate deed on the same date Elias gives John D. the, "privilege of building a dam across the creek in the same place where a dam was once commenced and raising a pond that may flow not to exceed one and a half acres – together with the privilege of ingress and regress through said premises at a convenient place from the highway to said dam forever."

The saw mill was run by Conklin Brothers until the death of Jacob on Oct. 21, 1881. Immediately, Nov. 2, 1881, it was leased to Daniel Woodford by Fanny M. and C. Fidelia Conklin. The lease allows Woodford to raise the saw mill dam to the height of "9 feet 2 inches above the rock on the east side of the waste gate" for the sole use of a mill pond. From the date of the lease, "a yearly rent or sum of 25 cents is to be paid in equal yearly payments. And it is agreed that if any rent shall be due and unpaid or if default shall be made in any of the covenants herein contained, then it shall be lawful for the said first parties to re enter said premises and to remove all persons therefrom."

On the Agricultural Census of 1855 this farm is listed with 75 acres improved land (cleared) and 25 acres unimproved (wooded). 40 acres were plowed, 15 acres of pasture, 20 acres of meadow from which 10 tons of hay were harvested. 5 acres of wheat were planted from which 60 bushels were harvested; 8 acres of oats from which 130 bushels were harvested; 4 acres of corn from which 200 bushels were harvested; 1 ½ acres of hemp produced 1400 lbs. The value of the farm was $4,000.; stock $275 and implements $120. The value of the house was given as $1200.

Following the death of Fanny Conklin the property was sold. In 1895 James Partridge completely rebuilt the saw mill and installed a circular saw.

There have been several owners of this property after 1894 and before purchase by the Morezak family.

(No. 3) House probably built by Daniel Conklin about 1855. It was later occupied by John Milton Conklin for the last twenty years of his life.

Miss Stanton called it "Brookside" (No. 3) by Henry Stanton. Grist Mill is visible through the trees at right.

"Brookside" (No. 3) taken downstream by Henry Stanton.

No.3 – Prior to recent study, it was believed that the house across the creek from the grist mill was built by Reuben Conklin when he purchased it from his uncle, Elias, in 1846. However, the house is not shown on the map drawn in 1852 but it is marked "D. Conklin" on the map drawn in 1859 and published the next year. Daniel Conklin married, shortly after 1855, a woman named Sarah. They are listed on the 1860 and 1865 Census without children. He died in 1872.

Probably at the death of Fanny Conklin when No. 4 was sold, J. Milton moved here. On the Census 1900 (U.S.) and 1905 (N.Y.S.) Florence Stanton was in his household as a housekeeper. It was mortgaged with the mill and sold by the Pompey Disciples Church to Albert Carley in 1919 for $450. On the Census of 1925 Carley, a tool maker aged 51, was here with his wife Louise, aged 54, living in Mrs. L.V. Clark's house.

Richard N. Wright of Syracuse acquired it and used it throughout the 1930's as a summer camp. He sold it to Ollie Sheremeta in the 1950's and it fell down.

(No. 1) The saw mill in June, 1901 as taken by Henry Stanton. The original mill on this site had an upright saw. In 1895 James Partridge rebuilt it with a circular saw.
Standing L. to R.: Carrie Morrison Partridge, Florence Stanton and James Partridge.

Earl Partridge and Arthur Morrison harvesting ice on the mill pond about 1902 or '03. The saw mill is in the background.

Snap shot of the saw mill as taken from the road about 1915 by Mabel F.E. Berry.

Mill Dam Overflow.

No.1 – Part of the saw mill dam at right (One of photographer Henry Stanton's "artistic" shots)

"Below the Mill Dam" photographed by Henry Stanton June, 1902.

*The old home (No. 5) of Elias Conklin, the original part on the left built about 1808.
In 1841 he sold to Isaac D. and in the 1880's to James Partridge. Now 6771 Chase Rd.   (Ruth Smith)*

No. 5 – The biographical sketch of Elias Conklin in the <u>Reunion & History of Pompey</u> (1875) says that he was, "commonly known as 'Boss Conklin', a carpenter and joiner by trade; was a large and successful farmer as well as a miller. He employed a large number of workmen and built houses and barns and did other mechanical work for his neighbors, such as making wagons, sleighs, carts, ploughs etc. At an early day he made very many coffins, sometimes for pay, sometimes when persons were poor without pay, and would assist in digging graves without charge, so great was his sympathy for the unfortunate…"

Elias had three daughters who married and lived nearby; two sons, one of whom died unmarried at age 28 and the other, Josiah D., who lived a mile down the road. (No. 9)

The farm upon which Elias first settled and lived until selling it to nephew Isaac D. in 1841 was supposed to contain 100 acres for $200. The tax roll of 1848 shows it as 90 acres, 87 in 1874 and 93 acres when owned by Jim Partridge in 1893. On the Agricultural Census of 1855 it contained 65 acres of "improved" land (cleared) and 30 acres "unimproved" (wooded).

Elias continued to own between 94 and 100 acres where he lived with his daughter Betsey, wife of Warren Butts. (No. 6) . He was in the Butts household in 1850 and died there in 1854 ae. 80. The house still stands directly across from the Berwyn "Maplewood" Cemetery.

Isaac D. Conklin, with wife Martha and daughter Abigail (b. 1839) lived in this old home and ran his cousin's saw mill some of the time. Daughter Abigail married Ira Clark and had a daughter, Ida, (b. 1858). Early in 1877 James Partridge (1856-1938) came from Saratoga County to work in the grist mill and in Dec. 1877 he married Ida Clark. Partridge purchased this place from his father-in-law and Ida died shortly thereafter, 1883. Dec. 1887 he married Carolyn Louise "Carrie" Morrison (1871-1955). She left the property to her grand-daughter, Ruth Bush Smith and husband VanBergen Smith. It is now marked 6771 Chase Rd.

(No. 6) Heber Butts house in Berwyn across from Berwyn Cemetery. Photo taken July, 1978.

No. 6 -- This is the house said to have been built by Elias Conklin for his son-in-law, Warner Butts (1798-1882), and wife Betsey Conklin Butts (1800-1872). Here Elias lived through the last thirteen years of his life. Warner Butts first appears on a tax roll in 1832 with 24 acres, 88 acres by 1846 and 134 acres after the death of his father-in-law. The Directory of 1868 found him running a saw mill.

Pompey Hill "Journal" correspondent Luella Dunham heard the tolling of the church bell on June 25, 1882. "For a long time the tolling of the church bell on the death of an individual has not been observed. The time-honored and appropriate custom seemed obsolete. When family friends chose to observe the usage in spite of modern indifference, their good sense in paying this just tribute to the departed is regarded with sincere respect. On Sunday afternoon the stillness was broken by the clear-toned church bell, reverberating over hill and vale for miles around, saying to the listening ear that 'The angel with the amaranthine wreath' had again visited some household. Mr. Warner Butts was called to go. Until the infirmities of age forbade, Mr. Butts was a regular attendant of the Presbyterian Church. A slight personal acquaintance with him leads to the belief he was of sunny, genial disposition. He led a quiet life on his farm near Conklin's Mills. No breath of suspicion ever tainted his reputation and there is every reason to believe he was an exemplification of the manly virtues."

According to the tax roll of 1893, after Warner Butts died his farm was owned in equal halves by his sons Homer (b. 1829) and Heber (b. 1834). Homer's wife died May 14, 1875. The Census of that year shows Heber with wife Abigail and children: Hattie (b. 1867), Warner (b. 1870) and Ella (b. 1875). It was Heber's little daughter Harriet, who was attacked in November, 1875.

"A MONSTROUS, PERFIDIOUS CRIME"
"A Terrible Outrage in Pompey
– A Tramp's Villainy –
He is Lodged in Jail"

"We have the details of a most horrible and sickening crime committed in the Town of Pompey (note: it was in LaFayette) on Tuesday, the 9th instant, but they are too indecent for publication. The principle facts are as follows: About a month ago, Heber Butts, residing about two miles southwest of Pompey Hill, took into his employ a young man aged about nineteen who gave the name of Charles Doyle and pretended to have a home in Niagara county. He was of that species of humanity commonly known as a tramp and told various stories about his past history. He claimed to have been a sailor but had become tired of such a life, and was desirous of engaging in agricultural pursuits. His labors were reasonably satisfactory to his employer, and no vicious traits in his character were even suspected till the occasion to which we are about to allude. It now transpires that he was a very bad person. A little daughter of Mr. Butts, eight years of age, told on Thursday at school what transpired on the Tuesday previous – a story which would almost cause the blood of a stoic to boil. Threatenings of severe punishment sealed the lips of the little sufferer until by accident evidences of the beastial outrage were discovered. But that is not all: the girl is now the victim of a most loathsome disease! The villain was arrested and taken before Justice VanBrocklin who committed him to the penitentiary to await the sitting of the grand jury next week. The order of the Justice was executed yesterday by Constable Peter Parslow. The inhuman wretch is sure to receive the full penalty of the law." *(Syracuse Journal, Nov. 13, 1875)*

"To the Editor of the Syracuse Journal: The excitement into which this community was thrown on Friday last by the report of a fiendish outrage upon the person of a little girl, aged only eight years, -notice of which has already appeared in the Journal – has partially subsided. At one time popular indignation reached a fever heat, and the inflamed populace threatened summary punishment to the brute who committed the foul deed. Even Judge Lynch was called into requisition shortly after the examination before Justice VanBrocklin was concluded. A crowd of men and large boys, carrying a coil of rope, besieged the headquarters of Constable Peter Parslow, yelling vociferously, and 'Hang him!', 'Kill him!' rent the air. But the officer sternly and firmly insisted that the law should be respected, and finally succeeded in quieting the enraged people. The first informant of this affair was slightly in error, when this occurrence was located in Pompey. The scene of the aggravated crime is about three miles from this village in a southwesterly direction, near Conklin's Mills, just over the line between this town and LaFayette, thus relieving us of the stigma." *(Journal, Nov. 18, 1875)*

THE POST OFFICE
Marionville 1878 – 1893
Berwyn 1893 - 1902

The farm house of Fruit Side, now 6983 Chase Rd. It was built by Israel and Lowley Woodford in 1818, raised to a full two story house in 1862. South wing added by Israel Lonzo Woodford in 1842. The Marionville post office was moved here about 1892 and the name changed to Berwyn Jan. 4, 1893 by Mrs. Cornelia Birdseye Woodford. She is standing with the horse in this picture.

The name "Marionville" was chosen when a post office was established for the Woodford Settlement, opened April 18, 1878 and named in honor of Francis Marion, the 'swamp fox' of Revolutionary War fame. "The new post office at Marionville, more generally known as Woodford Settlement is now in operation. From there a stage runs to the Summit Station. This does not seem to disturb E. Olcott who continues to accommodate passengers on the old line from Pompey to LaFayette." *(Syracuse "Courier", May 28, 1878)*

The name was changed to "Berwyn" January 4, 1893 upon the request of Cornelia Birdseye Woodford, wife of Lucien Woodford, who found it in a novel she was reading and thought it to be poetic. The new name was approved likely because the post office was located in Mrs. Woodford's sitting room, the farm called "Fruit Side" at the corner of Chase and Berwyn Roads.

Mrs. Cornelia Birdseye Woodford, left, with her niece and adopted daughter, Miss Ruth Estey Woodford (b. 1891).

Mrs. Cornelia Birdseye Woodford and her animals.

Another version as to how the name was put forward is by Roy E. Fairman, the Syracuse "Herald" roving reporter in 1930 or '31.

BERWYN, ONCE BUSY HAMLET, LIES IN RUINS
Mills Abandoned and Fallen to Pieces; Houses Vacant
ONCE MARIONVILLE
Post Office Name Later Changed to Berwyn, Given Up in 1902
By Roy E. Fairman, The Herald's Roving Reporter

"Within the areas of Central New York counties are scores of all but abandoned hamlets, many of which within the memory of men and women still living, were vying with other villages for places in the sun.

In some of them a few old houses are still standing, weather beaten and dilapidated, most of them unoccupied except by rats and bats. Others are in crumbling ruins and on still other sites where men and women with hearts aflame with hope and ambition founded homes, only ivy and weed-lined pits mark what once were cellars.

Upper Berwyn School at right, corner of Berwyn and Chase Rds. (Syracuse Post-Standard, June 18, 1933)

Onondaga County has many of these once thrifty and prosperous communities which have fallen by the wayside as modern business and modern conditions of life caused the tide of traffic to be diverted from them.

In the earlier years of the 19th century before the Civil War, Berwyn was such a hamlet, with ambitions to outgrow Fabius, Pompey, Apulia, LaFayette and other neighboring villages.

On the road trip from Pompey Hill to Apulia, now being rebuilt by Onondaga County, with mills nearby on the stream known as Conklin's Creek, with a cooperage, a cider making plant and an ax factory, Berwyn appeared destined to attain an important place among Onondaga County communities.

For many years farmers of goodly parts of the towns of Pompey, Fabius and LaFayette carried their grist to Conklin's mills, all of which have disappeared except parts of the dam and mill races which have survived the ravages of sun, wind and storm.

Sturdy trees grew on much of that territory and many farm houses which have housed families for three or four generations were built from lumber sawed from the log in the sawmill at Berwyn.

"Berwyn Mill Ruins"

In early days the milk from dairies in that part of Onondaga County was made into cheese or butter in the farm homes. Even when cheese factories began to take much of the milk, many farmers still made butter and wooden firkins were much in demand as were barrels for potatoes grown in large number.

In consequence, a cooperage thrived at Berwyn almost up to the present century and gave employment to many men. A cider mill, too, provided seasonal work as the farmers drew their apples to the mill and returned home with sweet apple juice.

As the hamlet grew into a busy settlement a post office was established there, the mail being taken there by stage from Onativia. The same stage then went on to Pompey Hill, which now obtains its mail by way of Jamesville.

The post office was at first called Marionville, but with so many "M'-villes", such as Martonville, Munnsville, Mannsville, etc., residents of Marionville found to their annoyance that mail frequently went astray, being sent by mistake to another village with name similar in appearance and sound.

After searching for a change in the post office name, one of the residents of Marionville returned from Berwyn, Ill., and the Marionville folk liked the name of the western village so well that the post office became "Berwyn".

During the latter part of the 19th century the village ran into sad days. Trees had been cleared from most of the land and a sawmill no longer operated there at a profit. Changes of farm practice led to the buying of more "patent" feed and the grist mill lost most of the trade.

Cheese factories absorbed more and more of the milk of that territory and butter making no longer created demand for firkins.

Then came rural free mail delivery. A route was established out of Fabius village covering the territory which had been cared for by the Berwyn post office and the post office was abandoned in 1902. Lucius Trowbridge, now dead, was the last postmaster. Preceding him was Raymond Swift, whose widow now lives in Cuyler with her son, the Rev. Carl Swift, pastor of Cuyler, Fabius and Keeney Settlement Methodist Episcopal Churches.

Changing times of the last 30 years have caused a gradual exodus from Berwyn and today that once thriving hamlet is virtually abandoned.

In the majority of deserted villages churches still stand. Berwyn never had a church building, but services were conducted each Sunday for many years in the district school house with pastors from Pompey preaching there." *(Syracuse Herald, probably 1930 or '31)*

Rev. Hiram V. Williams, Methodist minister at Summit Station 1891-1894, now Apulia Station, "will conduct religious services at the Berwyn school house on Monday evenings of each week." *(Standard, Jan. 26, 1894)* "The Society of Christian Work" was organized by the residents of Berwyn, and incorporated Jan. 30, 1907, to meet in the school house there."

MARIONVILLE IN 1883

"Daniel Woodford is Postmaster, carries on the sawmill business, grinds feed when the creek is high and if you wish blacksmithing done, he or his son 'Abe' will do it in a workmanlike manner. C. DuBois is deputy postmaster, has for sale tobacco and cigars, manufactures tubs, barrels, and the best butter packages made. Saturdays are his repair days. Bring on the old cast-off bung-holes and have nice new barrels made for them. Israel Woodford, the popular stage driver, carries the mail and makes regular morning and Saturday evening trips to Pompey and Onativia Station. He always makes 'schedule time' and can stow away, comfortably, more passengers in a given space than any other man in the business. J. Milton Conklin will furnish anything in the line of flour and feed or grind your grist 'while you wait'. If you wish a good wagon or sleigh made, or old ones repaired, call on Reuben Woodford. For the services of a first-class carpenter and joiner apply to William Clark or Frank Downing. If you wish to subscribe for the 'Tully Times' deposit the cold cash with Wells W. Swift and be made happy fifty-two times a year. When your threshing is ready, send for Seward Cook and his steam thresher and your poultry will find it impossible to fatten on the straw stack. If you wish to exchanges or purchase a good watch, H.W. Goodwin can furnish just the article desired. Everything in the line of nursery stock is supplied by Will A. Robbins or Lucian Woodford. Miss Clara Clark 'wields the birch' in our district school with universal satisfaction. Mrs. Robbins and Mrs. Hodges attend to the carpet weaving, Mrs. Mina Woodford to the dressmaking and Mrs. L.P. Case to the music teaching. *(Tully Times, August 4, 1883).* "Will Robbins is working for the LaFayette Manufacturing Company making bedroom furniture suites." (Tully Times, November 4, 1883)

Daniel Woodford in his blacksmith shop; the cooper shop was in the front part of the building. He died Jan. 29, 1908, ae. 83 yrs., 7 mos., and 8 days.

THE WOODFORD SCHOOL DISTRICT

An organizational meeting of the 15th school district of the Town of Pompey was held in the log cabin of Israel and Lowley Woodford October 19, 1814. Allen Hayden was chosen as moderator and Israel was the clerk and elected as one of the trustees. The other trustees were Elias Conklin and Thomas Grimes. The inhabitants of the district voted to raise $300. by tax for the purpose of building a school house; "to hire a teacher and set up a school to commence November 15, and continue four months." Parents of school children were "to procure one quarter of a cord of three foot wood for each Schollar delivered at the said Schoolhouse on or before the fifteenth day of December next". It was further, "moved and seconded that the School Master board with the Imployers and that the winter school be kept five months…" "Moved and seconded that the teacher Board with his employers in equal proportion to the Schollars sent…" "Voted that any man neglecting to get his quota of wood shall pay to the trustees for the same at the rate one Dollar per Cord and that none but hard wood be accepted."

The following are some of the votes taken at various annual and special meetings of the school district 1815 to 1950.

1815 – Voted that the Widow Alithear Butts be exonerated from paying her last summer's school bill.

1818 – Virgil Woodford is to make the fire in the school house and have the ashes. Truman Woodford has the same job and terms in 1823.

1819 – "Voted that we have a woman teacher for the summer term of May 1 to October 15. Voted to pay Harvey Woodford $39.75 for teaching the school 4 ½ months, Nov. 15 to April 1." (winter term)

1822 – Voted that the wood be cut and split so as to be suitable for the fire place. But the next year they specified that, "we get a half cord of wood to each scholar – three feet long corded at the school house and measured by the teacher and no logs accepted."

1824 – At the October annual meeting it was voted to have "an open stove for the school house…we to take the chimney down and convey it out of the house." Just two weeks later, however, at another meeting it was "voted that the vote taken for getting an open stove be reconsidered" and that "it be left in the hands of the trustees to get such a stove as they think proper… that we get a half of wood to every scholar 18 inches long split for a stove delivered and corded."

1825 – "Voted that we have a woman school teacher begin the first Monday in May next and continue for 20 weeks…Publius V. Woodford to continue the school during the (winter) season."

1826 – With formation of the town of LaFayette the districts of Pompey were re-numbered; this one was changed from #15 to #22. In 1831 it was changed again from #22 to

#17, joint with LaFayette. "Voted that whoever does not get their wood by the 10th day of January next shall pay 75 cents per cord."

1839 – "Voted to raise $20. And with other money the trustees have in their hands by subscription to purchase a school library; Marvin Wicks to take charge of the library books…every book shall be returned in four weeks…every book shall be kept within this district."

1842 – Resolved that the trustees build a privy for the benefit of the school children and that there be a tax of $15 raised for building a privy and repairs on the school house.

1845 – "Voted that the trustees expend the Library Money of $9.73 for a school apparatus such as globes, map, charts etc."

On September 25, 1845 it was voted 11 to 7 to build a new school house. To "enlarge the present site to half an acre, fenced with a good substantial fence." James VanBrocklin and Samuel P. Hayden who were both carpenters by trade and Harvey M. Woodford were named as a committee to submit a plan. Hayden presented its work three weeks later calling for a building 34 feet by 28 feet; an entry in the north end, 5 rows of seats and desks with six seats and desks in a row; a wood house 15 or 16 feet square and two privies. At an adjourned meeting on November 13, 1845 it was decided to cut the size of the building to 32 feet long and 24 feet wide; the wood house would be 16 feet long and 12 feet wide. The committee for construction was named as Harvey M. Woodford, Samuel P. Hayden, Truman Woodford, and Elias Conklin. The structure was to be completed by October 1, 1846.

The new house was completed and accepted by a unanimous vote of the tax payers on Nov. 5, 1846 at a cost of $340. Some incidental expenses noted were a broom 16₵, two foot scrapers 63₵, stove and pipe $7.06, one small bell 34₵, table $3.00, tin cup 10₵, two pounds of chalk.

1850 – Voted that the trustees get the school house insured with the Washington Mutual Insurance Co. and to raise $4.00 for the purpose of the said insurance.

1854 – Israel Lonzo Woodford to be the librarian, the library to be kept at the school house and to be opened for distribution of books every Saturday between the hours of twelve and one o'clock.

1862 – Resolved to get 15 cords of 18 inch wood to be fitted to the stove and corded in the yard. The wood contract was awarded to Ira Clark, lowest bidder, for 75₵ per cord. Resolved that we raise a tax of $15. to pay for the wood. The next year the lowest bidder was Daniel Woodford at $1.00 per cord.

1869 – "Special meeting ordered by the trustee March 22, for the purpose of considering the subject of some disorderly boys in said district. Voted that Frank Partridge and Thomas Kelly come forward and make confession of their faults and promise to do better for the future and be released from further censure, which was consented to and accepted."

1902 – The first female was elected to hold an office in the district – Fannie C. Swift elected clerk.

Jennie Partridge, born Feb. 1890.

Photo: Ruth Bush Smith

"GIRLS OF BERWYN"

by Henry Stanton, probably 1901

Back Row: Olive Sherman (b. 1894)
               Florence Robbins (b. 1889)
               Ruth Woodford (b. Jan., 1891)

Front (seated):
         Lucia Sherman (b. 1889)
         Clara Robbins
         Jennie Partridge (b. Feb., 1890)

UPPER BERWYN SCHOOL

Built 1846

Front Row seated (L to R): Iva Frost, Leslie Morrison, Carlena Cook
Second Row seated (L to R): James Kelly, Evelyn Bailey, Ernest Cramer
Standing at left (L to R): Paul Woodford, Mary Kelly, Ruth Woodford
Standing at right: (L to R): unknown boy with Teacher Agda Anderson
Third Row (L to R): Paul Swift, Carl Swift, Seward Cook, Clara Robbins
Back Row (L to R): Jennie Partridge, Florence Robbins

(Photo June 1905)

1931 – Vote on centralization of the district; with Fabius, 14 "No"-10 "Yes"; with Pompey, 17 "No"- 9 "Yes".

1937 – Voted 11 to 10 to transport 8th grade and high school students to Fabius Central School.

1947 – Voted to contract with Fabius Central School for all grades.

1950 – Voted to centralize the district with Fabius Central School. An auction of the school contents to be held June 15, 1950. Real estate to revert to the original owner or successor, now known as Charles Jenner. The property was sold to Merwin Brown May 2, 1957.

"Record of the School Meetings of the Woodford District School from its formation Oct. 19, 1814 to its dissolution May 31, 1950" *(Transcribed by J. Roy Dodge for Sylvia Shoebridge, April, 2007. The original is in the Onondaga Historical Assn. as of 1950)*

THE WOODFORD SETTLEMENT

Israel Woodford (1770-1852) and Lowley Woodford (1775-1860), his cousin and wife, were married in Farmington, CT in 1794 where the family had lived for over one hundred years. They had ten children, the first three born in Farmington. Early in 1801 they moved to Edinburg, Saratoga County, New York where they remained ten years and their next four children were born. In 1811 they removed to Pompey, NY. They came with a team of oxen and settled on fifty acres along both sides of what is now Chase Rd. They built a log cabin facing on the south side of Chase Rd. where they lived for seven years. In 1818 they built a one story frame house across Chase Rd. facing Berwyn Rd. Thirty more acres were purchased in 1815. Their son Romanta was married at that time and moved into the log cabin until his own frame house was built.

In 1841 their youngest son, Israel Lonzo (1816-1903) bought the farm from his parents with 101 acres. He built an addition onto the south side of the house in time for his marriage the next year to Pamelia Northrup (1819-1907), daughter of Abraham Northrup. In 1862 the old central chimney and fireplaces were removed from the house and the roof raised making a full second story. In 1895 Israel L. and Pamelia sold the farm to their son, Lucien L. (1859-1927). In 1916 he sold it out of the family and moved to Syracuse.

The historical sermon by Rev. Jeremiah Petrie of the Pompey Congregational (Presbyterian) Church, July 2, 1876, recalled Israel. "Israel Woodford united with this church by letter from the church in Farmington, Conn., Sept. 1812; was chosen deacon of this church April 4, 1818. In earnest and active piety he seems to have excelled all the offices and members of the church whose memory comes down to us today. There is a hallowed sweetness in his life which still sheds its fragrance, and may its godly savor ever remain."

Ansel Woodford, right, was photographed at the home of his daughter, Delia Woodford Morrison, widow of James, within the year before his death in 1904, aged 87. Seated on the left is Hervey Woodford Morrison (1868-1914) son of Delia; his son Abram (b. Jan. 1897) and Delia seated in the middle. The house is now numbered 1929 Berwyn Rd. *(Photo: Ruth Bush Smith)*

All ten of the Woodford children spent their lives in or near their settlement. The six sons were Harvey Munson (1795-1876); Romanta (1797-1880); Amon Whitfield (1799-1884); Publius Virgil (1802-1896); Truman Osman (1807-1883); Israel Lonzo ((1816-1903). All owned farms, mostly on Lots #78 and #93. The girls were: Emily Augusta (1804-1883); Maria Ann (1810-1838); Lowley Emiline (1813-1892) and Sarah Fitch (1819-1901).

Lucien L. Woodford compiled the genealogy over several years, completing it in 1924. On March 1, 1925 he dated his "Sketch of the Woodford Colony, Pompey, NY" by which he described 24 properties owned by family descendants, mostly along Berwyn Rd. and surroundings. It is from his compilations that this sketch is composed.

THE WOODFORD CHEESE FACTORY

1874-1881

The first American cheese factory is said to have been opened in Connecticut in 1844. But it was not until the late 1860's that cheese factories were started in Central New York. The opportunity of securing a marketable sale for their milk, then largely confined to the months of May to November, was especially welcome and innovative to farmers. In some factories the farmers took their payment in the product and sold it themselves. At others an Association was formed to sell the cheese through commission agents. When fluid milk and its products could be shipped in ice packed railroad cars beginning about 1888, the small local factories were soon put out of business.

The Pompey correspondent to the Syracuse "Journal" announced on May 26, 1874 that, "another new cheese factory has been erected, near the residence of Alonzo M. Woodford in the Woodford Settlement. It is nearly finished and will be ready for business in about two weeks." (Lot 93 – now southeast corner of Chase and Collins Roads.)

"Woodford's cheese factory at Marionville is establishing a reputation for the manufacture of the best cheese that can be found in the markets anywhere. Mr. Ansel Woodford is to be congratulated on his success as a cheese maker." (*Journal, Aug. 8, 1878*)
"Mr. Ansel Woodford, of the Woodford Cheese Factory, is rapidly gaining the reputation of being one of the leading cheese makers in the state. His factory thus far has sold more cheese and has received better prices than any of the others around here. Eight cents per pound was received for cheese last week. This factory supplies the leading grocers at Syracuse." (*Journal, Aug. 21, 1878*)

The Woodford factory burned to the ground March 12, 1881 and was not rebuilt.

FRUIT SIDE FARMING

Ideas and Energy
Worked Into an Old
Pompey Farm
A Promising Fruit and Nursery
Business --- Success in Marketing

The "Fruit Side" Farm at the corner of Chase and Berwyn Roads. At right, Lucien and Cornelia Birdseye Woodford with Lucien's mother, Pamelia Northrup Woodford (Mrs. Israel Woodford).

"Away in the southwest corner of Pompey, six miles from the Delaware, Lackawanna & Westerm Railroad at Summit or at Onativia, is the hamlet of Berwyn, formerly known as Marionville. Before these names were given to the place for post office purposes the locality was known as the Woodford neighborhood. A school was established there many years ago, and about the same time a blacksmith shop, and on both sides of the road for a distance of two and one half miles rows of maple trees were set which today are great bouquets of red and gold. Israel Woodford had six sons and three daughters (sic) all of whom married and settled upon adjoining farms on the Woodford road and planted the maple trees. The school and the smithy were principally for their use. Changes came during 50 years and most of the families have gone from the neighborhood and the state, leaving no successors of their name but letting the land pass to other occupants.

"Why don't he come?"
Photo taken in June 1901 by Henry Stanton.

Looking south on Berry Rd. in front of the John Berry farm, right side of road, and Will Haviland farm left side, which he occupied 1881-1913.

(Sylvia Shoebridge)

One of the brothers who remained was Israel L. Woodford whose farm of about 100 acres lay upon the east side of the road, opposite the school. This was the original homestead of his father's planting and there he was born in 1816. He has lived there ever since, never having been off the place for a longer time than five weeks. He has been a good farmer in his day and an excellent citizen, but age crept upon him year by year, robbing him of energy and courage, and the time came when he was disposed to give up the management of the farm. Of his two children one was a son, Lucien L., a young man of slight physique, nervous temperament and quick perception. When Mr. Woodford proposed selling the farm Lucien made an offer to buy and to the astonishment of his father produced almost enough money to pay for it. The fund he had been saving up from childhood, mostly from wages earned after the age of 21 on the farm and as a teacher. The farm became his and he has been exercising upon it some of his new ideas, for he clearly perceived years ago that old ways would have to give place to new ones, and the sooner he got out of the rut of general farming the more benefit there would be for him in the new era to come. Dairying had ceased to pay; grain and hay could no longer be depended upon for profit and the market was too far away.

Mr. Woodford had observed that farmers round about devoted little or no attention to the production of summer vegetables and fruits, but most of them would buy whenever they had opportunity. Here was an idea worth putting to the test and he proceeded forthwith to plow up the old pasture land which had not been disturbed by cultivation more than once in a generation. The neighborhood was astonished, not to say shocked, when the furrows were turned and more so when fence after fence was attacked and carted away to the wood pile or the lumber stack. After the land had been worked into suitable condition by cropping to vegetables it was planted to berry bushes, red and black and yellow raspberries of the best kinds of the day, and a considerable orchard of plums.

Year by year judicious additions have been made including currants, cherries, grapes, pears, blackberries and many more plums. In the meantime expenses were kept up chiefly by vegetables which were grown to perfection in the deep rich soil of the old pasture and were said to advantage in the surrounding country. Asparagus has been included on a moderate scale and has paid relatively as well as any crop in the list. This year has brought out a full yield of fruit on many of the vines and trees and while the season has been an unfortunate one for the profitable sale of such produce it has given the opportunity for developing the important faculty of finding a market for what you have produced.

Mr. Woodford's books are private and he is not disposed to parade before the people what he has accomplished in a business way, but a few points of particular interest have been learned that may be disclosed. A bed of Snyder blackberries, bearing this year for the second time, yielded over 80 bushels of fruit, by reason of excellent quality and careful sorting, brought the highest price from people who appreciate merit. You may set it down at ten cents a quart throughout. The ground was five-eighths of an acre.

A few years ago a new variety of raspberries was announced by Mr. Thompson of Oneida Castle. It was a combination of the red and black sorts, having many excellent points but unpopular because of the color. Lucien Woodford looked into the matter and decided to put some money into a few hundred plants of the Columbias. He is very well pleased with his investment, for the new sort has surpassed all others upon his grounds in every profitable respect. The weakness of color he overcomes by a little argument with the trade. A trial quart of the fruit is given to each customer and in every case they order these berries in preference to any others. An idea as to its productiveness may be gathered from the fact that Mrs. Woodford picked four and one half quarts from a single bush at one picking.

Plums have been a drug in the fruit market this fall, and hundreds of bushels have gone to waste for lack of buyers. In some parts of Onondaga and Oswego counties you could buy all the plums you wanted for 25 cents a bushel on the trees. The Woodfords, six miles from a railroad, with the villages of Tully, Cortland and Homer the nearest markets, overloaded with the fruit and likewise Syracuse, had 100 bushels of plums to find buyers for. That was no easy problem. But they didn't wait for the fruit to ripen before setting to work on its solution. Out in Ohio they found a section of the country without a supply of plums. In Oberlin prices were obtained and a trial shipment was made. The express rate was $1.75 per 100 pounds, more than double the general price of the fruit in Syracuse. The plums were put up in neat baskets and sent forward. Satisfactory sales led to further shipments and the bulk of the crop went in that way. It was a complete success and the net price received at Berwyn was $1.27 a bushel. Pluck and ideas were all rewarded, and so satisfactory was the transaction with the commission agent and the customers that the Berwyn fruit can go to Oberlin again whenever it is ready.

The selling of superior fruit led easily to inquiries for plants and this was the beginning of a new line of business. Three years ago the Woodfords began on a small scale to furnish nursery stock to a few score of inquirers. A moderate amount of advertising and the issue of a small catalog of varieties precipitated an unexpected demand last year for nursery stock, including flowers and shrubs. Undoubtedly their remarkable display of flowers at last year's county fair contributed to this result. It is safe to say that no such collection of gladioluses, asters and sweet peas was ever before shown in Syracuse.

Mr. Woodford is fitting himself for a larger scope in horticulture by attending the agricultural school of Cornell University whenever he can spare a few weeks or day, and Prof. Roberts has shown his interest in the enterprises of his pupil by visiting the place and in many other ways.

Mr. Woodford's partner in his business and his home is a lady of remarkable executive ability and tact, and a favorite in society. She is a daughter of Albert F. Birdseye, and grand-daughter of the original Victory Birdseye, one of the leading pioneers citizens of Pompey. She is thoroughly interested in the development of the business and has contributed her full share toward the results attained. Even in the matter of finding and testing Markets, Mrs. Woodford has done most intelligent and skillful work. It was through her instrumentality that the name of the post office was changed, for good business reasons but against the wish of the general community, although all are now content. The name given to the farm and nursery, Fruit Side, is most appropriate, unless the great and growing flower gardens shall in time come to overshadow the fruit business. The prospect for a large development of both the fruit and the nursery business is at present very good. A possible extension is also suggested by the frequent demands from Syracuse families for quantities of fruit put up in glass cans for home use.

The Woodfords have made many useful discoveries in the way of doing work and have adopted any number of labor saving devices; but they have not yet discovered any genuine substitute for work and they are as busy people as the town of Pompey contains. Mr. Woodford can turn his hand to many mechanical trades and has the facilities for making and mending all manner of tools. He has constructed a system of waterworks for the farm, house, gardens and fountains; built a small greenhouse, made extensive changes in all his buildings. In fact he has completely transformed the old farm. To make the business pay he finds that waste must be reduced to a minimum, and even the decaying plums are turned to account by building a temporary fence around the orchard and turning in a drove of pigs.

But life at Fruit Side is not a continuous business whirl. There is a social side to it. The fine old house is a center of refinement and humane feeling. Literature, art and religion abide there and dominate the household as well as the business of the place. Both Mr. and Mrs. Woodford are members of the Grange, Patrons of Husbandry, and have been prominent supporters of the Grange at Pompey. They are also members of the old Congregational church, Mr. Woodford being an elder and Mrs. Woodford a most popular teacher in the Sunday school. With their abundant and ceaseless duties they find time for the enjoyment of life's privileges at home and in quite extensive travel." (*Syracuse "Standard", Oct. 26, 1897*)